Greenhaven World History Progra

GENERAL EDITORS

Malcolm Yapp
Margaret Killingray
Edmund O'Connor

Cover design by John Castle

ISBN 0-89908-124-X Paper Edition
ISBN 0-89908-149-5 Library Edition

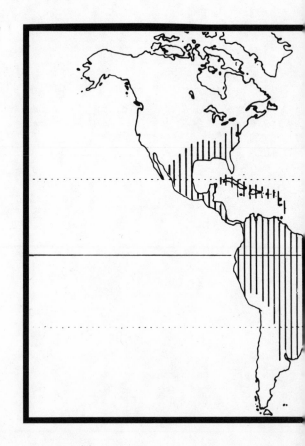

THE SLAVE TRADE

by David Killingray

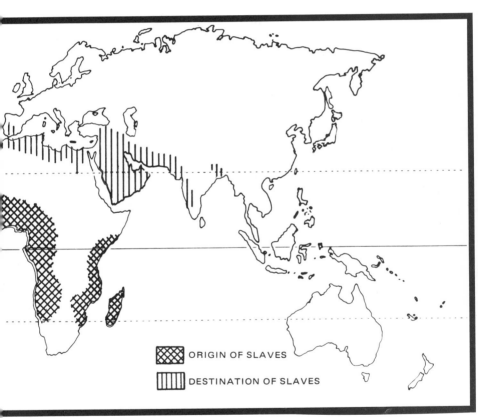

⬚ ORIGIN OF SLAVES

⬚ DESTINATION OF SLAVES

Greenhaven Press, Inc.
577 SHOREVIEW PARK ROAD
ST. PAUL, MN 55112

The slave market in Zabid, Yemen, in the thirteenth century showing African slaves being bought and sold by Arab traders

INTRODUCTION

One day in 1756 on the coast of West Africa an eleven-year-old black boy named Olaudah Equiano was sold to a British slave trader. Beaten and terrified, Olaudah was taken on board a ship and pushed into the stinking hold along with dozens of other slaves. (D1)* This was the brutal experience of nearly ten million Africans — men, women, and children — who, over a period of 350 years (1520-1870) were seized from Africa and carried across the Atlantic to America where they were forced to work as slaves.

SLAVERY

There have always been dirty, dangerous or unpleasant jobs which men did not want. How could they get others to do them? One modern way is to pay people enough money to persuade them to do these jobs. For most of history the usual way was to force them. So there have always been *slaves* — people who belonged to someone else and did what they were told.

What sort of jobs did slaves do? In the earliest times they were servants in the houses of rich men. In ancient Greece they could be

2   *The reference (D) indicates the numbered documents at the end of the book.

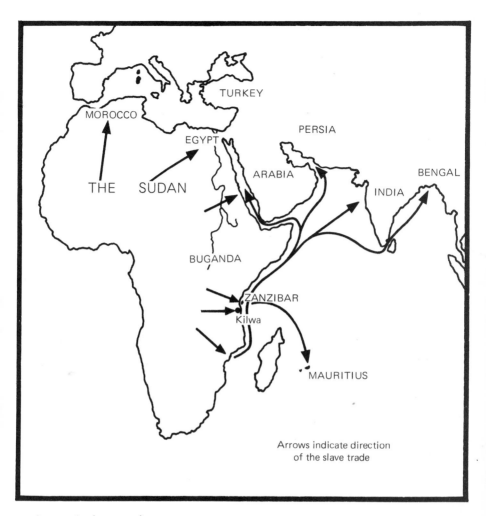

The Arab slave trade

found as workmen or in any job which required taking orders from someone else. In ancient Rome they worked in the great silver mines and farmed the huge estates. (D2) In the Muslim Middle East they did these jobs, but they also served as soldiers (never a popular job — that is why many countries have conscription) or as government officials. So some of the great Muslim empires were run by slaves. Slaves — men who belonged to the Sultan — held all the top jobs in the Ottoman Empire. In Egypt a similar system lasted for 250 years. Turkish slaves were brought from the Black Sea by ship to Egypt and trained as soldiers. They were called Mamluks and the Mamluks governed Egypt from the middle of the thirteenth century until the beginning of the fifteenth. At the end of the fifteenth century the black slaves of Bengal in India set

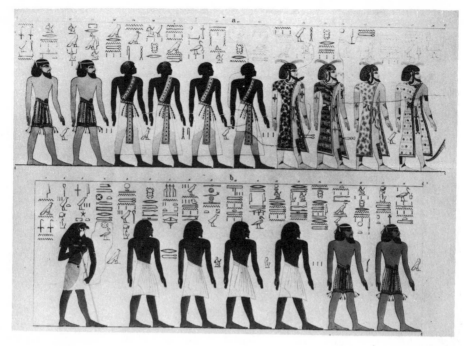

Slaves from many lands: an ancient Egyptian fresco. Slaves were taken from Africa even at the time of the Pharaohs.

up an independent kingdom. (D3)

How did men obtain slaves? The oldest way was to go out and capture them in war. This is the way the Arabs took theirs in the years of the great Arab conquests. Later the Arabs took most of their slaves from Africa and organized a large export of slaves from East Africa to Arabia, India and Iran, and from the western Sudan to the Mediterranean. Another method was to breed slaves, forcing slaves to have children who could take their places. A third method was to buy slaves. Often people wanted to be slaves. This sounds silly but you must remember that at least slaves were fed. A man without food might decide that it was better to sell himself and his

family into slavery rather than starve to death. In China, even two thousand years ago, people had decided this. In some places where slaves could rise to high positions parents were even anxious to sell their children as slaves.

For thousands of years there have been slaves and there has been slave trading. In this booklet, however, we are going to look at just one slave trade, the African slave trade in the sixteenth to nineteenth centuries. We have chosen this trade for three reasons. First, we know more about it. Second, it was bigger, more organized and had greater effects than any other. Third, it was different. The African slave trade was different in two ways. First, it

		%
North America	427,000	4·5
Spanish America - Mexico, Peru, Argentina	1,552,100	14·0
Brazil	3,646,800	38·0
Caribbean - Dutch, French, Danish, Spanish, British islands	3,765,200	42·0
Europe	50,000	·5
Atlantic islands - Sao Tome, Azores	125,000	1·0
TOTAL	9,566,100	100·0

Estimated slave landings 1520-1870

Slaves mining gold in Brazil

was the product of a world market. A world market means specialization. One form of specialization is the production of food and raw materials in plantations. Whereas in older times slaves did many jobs, in America they were needed mainly for one job, plantation labour. Second, the problem of slavery became mixed up with that of race and colour prejudice. In older times slaves were treated in many ways as if they were free men, except that they were slaves when they worked: when they ceased to work they could mix with others. Of course there were exceptions; some Arabs thought blacks were inferior. (D4) But in the African slave trade all the slaves were black and the owners were white. So the whites came to look on the blacks as inferior. We still see the results of this prejudice.

THE START OF THE TRANS-ATLANTIC SLAVE TRADE

Since the time of ancient Egypt slaves have been taken from Africa. For hundreds of years Arabs bought and sold black slaves, but the big increase in the slave trade came with the Europeans after 1600. The first Europeans to visit the west coast of Africa were Portuguese sailors in the mid-fifteenth century. They captured or bought slaves and sent them by sea to Portugal. (D5) Neither the Portuguese nor their African trading partners thought slavery was wrong. West Africa was seen

5

West African Trading Fort. It was to forts like this that the slaves were taken to be sold to the European traders.
Cape Coast Castle, 1682

as just another place with which to trade.

Between 1492 and 1520 the Spaniards discovered and conquered the West Indian islands and large parts of Central and South America. *(Columbus*)* The Europeans built settlements and began to exploit the wealth of the New World. Gold and silver from mines in the Andes Mountains and sugar from new plantations in Brazil were exported to Europe. American Indians (Amerindians) were forced to work as slaves by the white men but they died rapidly from harsh treatment and European diseases. Faced with a labour shortage the settlers began to import cheap, strong slaves — young men and boys known as 'prime slaves' — from West Africa.

Africans had a greater resistance to European diseases and they proved to be better workers than the Amerindians.

By 1650 most of the coastal states of Europe had possessions in America. There were Spaniards in Central and South America; Dutch and Portuguese in Brazil; English and French in the West Indies and North America. They all imported slaves from Africa.

During the seventeenth and eighteenth centuries more and more people in Europe began to use tropical goods such as sugar, tea, coffee, tobacco, cotton, and indigo which was used for making dyes. In America these crops were grown on plantations worked by many slaves. As the plantations increased so did the numbers of

*Titles in brackets refer to other booklets in the Program

Gang of captive slaves being marched to the coast

slaves brought from Africa.

The Europeans who traded with West Africa also bought gold, ivory and spices, but by the seventeenth century slaves had become the most important item of trade. When the Portuguese found they couldn't buy enough slaves they took them by force. (D6)

SLAVING IN WEST AFRICA

By 1700 most European countries took part in the slave trade with West Africa. Along the West African coast European trading companies built forts. In each fort trade goods were stored ready to be exchanged for the slaves and other goods supplied by the African rulers and merchants. West Africa was hot and very unhealthy, especially for Europeans. Many whites died of diseases, and by the nineteenth century the West African coast was popularly known as the 'white man's grave'. Life in the forts for the merchants, clerks and soldiers was uncomfortable and boring.

Local African kings and merchants were the trading partners of the Europeans. They lived in mud and thatch houses straggling beyond the walls of the fort. Slaves were exchanged for the iron, rum, woollen cloth and guns brought from Europe. The wealth of African rulers increased with the slave trade and some became very powerful. They commanded armies, controlled the trade routes to the coast, and supplied the forts with food. If one group of Europeans cheated them they could take their trade to another rival group. On other occasions they seized the fort and took over the trade with visiting European ships. The white trader had to be on good terms with the local African king. At Whydah, on the Slave Coast, the Dutch trader, William Bosman, respected the king and treated him fairly. By doing this he was able to gain valuable trading advantages over his English and French rivals.

In West Africa slaves were

African merchants selling slaves to the European traders. This picture shows clearly the cruelty of the slave trade.

Chained slaves being forced into the hold of a slave ship

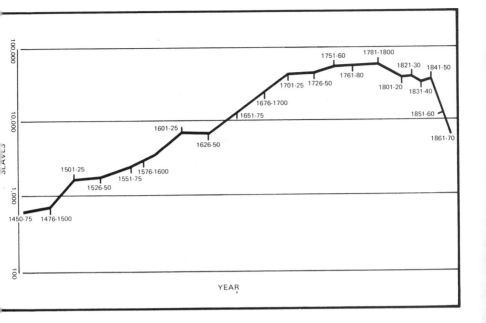

SLAVES

100,000

10,000

1,000

100

YEAR

1450-75 1476-1500

1501-25

1526-50

1551-75

1576-1600

1601-25

1626-50

1651-75

1676-1700

1701-25 1726-50

1751-60

1761-80

1781-1800

1801-20

1821-30 1841-50

1831-40

1851-60

1861-70

Graph to show the volume of the transatlantic slave trade 1450-1870

assembled at inland markets, chained together to prevent escape, and then marched in long columns over distances up to four hundred miles to the coast. (D7) Many of the slaves were prisoners-of-war, criminals, or people who owed money.

Some African states such as Ashanti and Dahomey went to war to capture slaves, using firearms bought from the Europeans. At the coast the slaves were bought by local African merchants and kings — the middlemen — who then exchanged them with the white traders at the fort. Bargaining was usually done in Portuguese, English or French for white men rarely took the trouble to learn an African language. Few African merchants could read or write but this didn't give Europeans all the advantages. William Bosman

recorded that 'the Negroes are accurate in their trade accounts working out sums of several thousands in their heads without the assistance of pen or ink'. Much of the trade was by direct barter. Bars of iron and smooth, white cowrie shells imported from the Indian Ocean were used as currency; in 1700 four thousand cowries threaded together on a string were worth about a quarter of an ounce of gold, or one English gold sovereign. As the slaves were bought they were branded and then locked in the fort to wait for the ship which would take them to America.(D8)

THE MIDDLE PASSAGE

The journey across the Atlantic to America was known as the middle

9

passage. When the weather was good it took between five and eight weeks. Sometimes rough seas or lack of wind made the journey much longer. The ship on which Olaudah Equiano was carried to the West Indies took almost twice as long, and food and water ran short. Slave ships, or slavers, varied in size from fifty to four hundred tons. The male and female slaves were separated from each other and packed into separate holds 'like books upon a shelf', or, as one captain put it, 'with not so much room to move as a man in his coffin'.

Troublesome slaves were kept in chains and only let on to the deck a few at a time for exercise. To keep the slaves as healthy as possible the crew would whip them to make them dance during exercise time. In desperation some slaves tried to jump overboard. To prevent this nets were hung around

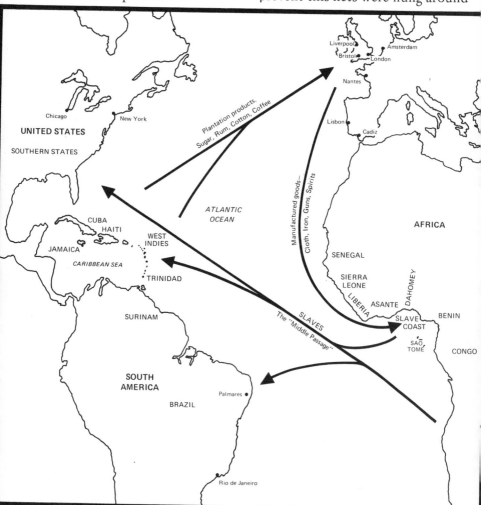

The transatlantic (triangular) slave trade

the deck. Many slaves died during the middle passage from harsh treatment, poor food, and disease. So did many of the crew. John Newton, a slave captain in the eighteenth century, estimated that a quarter of the slaves died; a recent estimate for the eighteenth century puts the figure at about 16%.

At the end of the middle passage the slaves were fed several good meals and shaved and washed in fresh water. Their bodies were then rubbed over with olive oil to make their skins shine so that they would look as healthy as possible when they were put up for sale.

THE TRIANGULAR TRADE

Slave trading with Africa was a risky but very profitable business. The 'triangular trade' brought great wealth to investors in Europe and America. A few Africans also grew rich. It was called the 'triangular trade' because the ships made three journeys which formed the three sides of a triangle. Goods made in the workshops of Europe were shipped to the West African coast where they were exchanged for slaves. The slaves were taken to America and sold at a large profit. In American ports the slavers would load goods such as sugar, rum, cotton and tobacco which had been produced by slave labour. These would then be shipped to Europe and sold at a further profit. British ships dominated this triangular trade.

On a voyage in 1767 the Liverpool slaver *Thomas* made an overall profit of £24,000 although a hundred of the 630 slaves died before the ship reached Kingston in Jamaica. At that time a workman in Britain might earn less than five shillings for a week's work, so this was a very large profit indeed. Ports such as Liverpool, Bristol and London in Britain, Bordeaux and Nantes in France, Amsterdam in Holland, Lisbon in Portugal and Cadiz in Spain were crowded with the masts of slavers. One writer said of Liverpool: 'The great wealth from the trade in slaves fills the whole town, increasing the fortunes of the merchants and of the majority of the inhabitants.' No wonder that one enemy of the slave trade said that in Liverpool the 'bricks of the houses are cemented together by the blood of African slaves'.

WHITE JUSTIFICATIONS FOR THE SLAVE TRADE

Few whites in the seventeenth or eighteenth centuries saw anything wrong in enslaving black men. John Newton, a devout Christian who later became an opponent of the slave trade, wrote in the diary which he kept on his slaving voyages: 'Wednesday 21 March 1753. I thank God for an easy and creditable way of life'.

The first Europeans in Africa treated black men with respect. However, by the seventeenth century most white men had come to believe that Africans were inferior. Many whites believed that the Bible said God had cursed Africans to be 'servants forever', and that they were black because of their sins.

...aves cutting sugar cane on a plantation.
...s there were no machines to perform this
...rt of work, the wealth of the plantation
...vners depended on their having a vast
...nount of very cheap labour

Britain, men said, the continued prosperity and power of the country rested on the goods produced by blacks in America. (D9) Even when the British had ended the slave trade and slavery in their own colonies in the nineteenth century the Lancashire cotton towns continued to grow richer on cotton produced by slave labour in the United States.

SLAVERY IN THE AMERICAS

At the end of the middle passage the black slaves were unloaded and sold at American ports. It was common for slaves to be auctioned. This meant that they were put on show and examined by the customers like horses or cattle at a fair. They were sold to the person who bid the highest price.

Black slaves in America were items of private property; one slave law called them 'chattels personal'. Their masters regarded them as inferior creatures who could be bought and sold in the same way as pieces of furniture or farm animals. Families could be split up never to see each other again. (D10) The slave's value depended upon his or her use as a worker on the plantation, in the workshop or home. Although there were poor whites in America only blacks were slaves. Through their laws and the church the whites made it clear to the slaves who had the power. (D11)

New slaves had to be 'seasoned', that is, broken in to their work, and taught to be obedient to their masters. During this time many more blacks died. Disobedience

Another argument used to support the slave trade was that whites could not work in the heat of the tropics. This was nonsense because in the seventeenth century there were many white convicts and indentured labourers (poor whites who had agreed to work several years for low pay) working alongside blacks in the tropical parts of America. The main justification for the slave trade was that it was profitable. Wealthy sugar planters in the West Indies depended upon slave labour. In

TO BE SOLD, on board the Ship *Bance-Ijland*, on tuefday the 6th of *May* next, at *Ajhley-Ferry*; a choice cargo of about 250 fine healthy **NEGROES**, juft arrived from the Windward & Rice Coaft. —The utmoft care has already been taken, and fhall be continued, to keep them free from the leaft danger of being infected with the **SMALL-POX**, no boat having been on board, and all other communication with people from *Charles-Town* prevented.

Auftin, Laurens, & Appleby.

N. B. Full one Half of the above Negroes have had the SMALL-POX in their own Country. .

An advertisement for the sale of slaves, eighteenth century

was punished by the whip, chaining, and even *mutilation* — that is, being branded or having ears or feet cut off. 'Slaves must obey at all times. Negroes become unhappy if they are given too much freedom; complete submission is the only way with slavery', said a Virginia slave-owner. The slaves worked as labourers, seamen, carpenters, house servants, clerks, and factory workers. Some slaves, particularly in Brazil, served as soldiers. During the wars of independence in South America many slaves were given their freedom if they joined the army.

The majority of slaves worked on the plantations. The main plantation crop in the West Indies and Brazil was sugar; cotton and tobacco were grown in the southern United States. Slaves rarely left the plantations which were like a separate world. On large plantations several hundred blacks were employed in the fields, cutting cane or picking cotton. There were also many skilled jobs which were much sought after. (D12-13) The

Opponents of the slave trade produced pictures showing the brutal treatment of slaves

Capture of Nat Turner. His short bloody rebellion failed and he was hanged in a town called Jerusalem

wealthy owner lived in a mansion, or the 'big house' as the slaves called it, and left the daily running of the estate to a white overseer. Some overseers treated the slaves badly. 'It is essential to make the slaves stand in fear', said a slave owner. Not all slave owners were brutal. Many regarded their slaves like children who needed persuasion, kind treatment but firm control and correction. It is said that the most brutal slave owners were probably the Dutch and the English.

Throughout North and South America small groups of white men dominated the slave-owning communities. The most powerful whites were the owners of the large plantations – the 'planters'. In the British West Indian islands the 'planters' were so wealthy that they could influence what happened in Parliament three thousand miles away in London. And in the southern states of what is now the USA, although only a minority of the whites owned slaves they had most of the money and controlled the government in each state.

The life of the slave was controlled by slave laws, or codes. All these laws stressed that the black man, whether he was a slave or had gained his freedom, was a 'race distinct and inferior'. Some blacks even came to believe this absurd idea. Marriage between blacks and whites was illegal in most slave-owning colonies but many slave owners kept black mistresses. Thus throughout America there was a steadily growing number of people of mixed race.

SLAVE RESISTANCE AND REVOLT

How did blacks react to slavery? In Africa they fought against those who tried to capture them. And at sea the slaves sometimes revolted and seized the slave ship. In America some slaves just accepted their position. Many protested in the easiest way they could. They pretended to be stupid and not to understand orders; they worked slowly and broke machinery on purpose. In many ways the slave could be very 'troublesome property'. Some slaves were even bolder and more desperate and either escaped or plotted revolt. Those who escaped could expect to be hunted down and if caught punished severely. Slaves therefore fled into the swamps, forests and mountains. In the mountainous 'cockpit country' of central Jamaica and the forests of Surinam escaped slaves were able to live an independent life and even enter into treaties with the Europeans. In Brazil bands of blacks set up an independent republic at Palmares and for most of the seventeenth century defied Dutch and Portuguese attempts to overthrow it. (D14)

A constant fear of slave owners was a revolt by their slaves. Many slave risings took place throughout the American colonies but very few had effective leadership. They were short-lived outbursts of violence and destruction which were soon crushed by the better armed and organized whites. (D15) The only successful revolt was in the West Indian island of San

Toussaint l'Ouverture (1743-1803)

Domingo. Toussaint L'Ouverture, a former slave who led the rising, was influenced by the ideas of the French Revolution. He was a brilliant general and his victories over Spanish and French armies helped to create the first independent black republic of Haiti. (D16)

THE ABOLITION OF THE SLAVE TRADE

During the late eighteenth century there was a growing demand in Europe and North America to end the cruel slave trade. More and more people began to think of Africans as fellow human beings. (D17) Britain at this time was changing from a farming to an

Household slaves dressed in their best being inspected at a sale in New Orleans, 19th century

industrial country. Her trading interests were also changing. She had lost control of the trade of North America when her colonists had successfully revolted in the 1770s to set up the United States; and her trade with India and East Asia was growing. The 'sugar island' colonies of the West Indies became steadily less important to Britain and her new manufacturers noticed the continued influence of the West Indian planters. Many merchants supported free trade and argued that slavery was an inefficient way

Pro-slavery pictures in the United States showed the black slave as happy and carefree

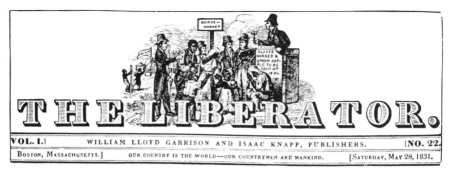

THE LIBERATOR.

VOL. I.]   WILLIAM LLOYD GARRISON AND ISAAC KNAPP, PUBLISHERS.   [NO. 22.

BOSTON, MASSACHUSETTS.]   OUR COUNTRY IS THE WORLD—OUR COUNTRYMEN ARE MANKIND.   [SATURDAY, MAY 28, 1831.

The front page of 'The Liberator', the anti-slavery newspaper founded by William Lloyd Garrison in the United States in 1831

to produce goods. (D18) The idea that all human beings should be given equal rights was put forward by writers. Anti-slavery societies were formed in Britain and France to try to end the slave trade. Denmark was the first country to make the slave trade illegal; the French revolutionary government in 1794 freed all the slaves in the French empire but Napoleon later restored slavery. In Britain the Anti-Slavery Society was well organized with supporters in parliament. (D19) It helped to free black slaves brought to Britain. In 1807 a new law made it illegal for British people to buy slaves in Africa. The United States passed a similar law in 1808. Other European countries slowly followed. It must be remembered that this was only the start of the end of the slave trade, *not* of

A print from an Anti-Slavery Society publication showing Britannia as protectress of the slaves

slavery. Slaves were still bought and sold in the United States and in most European colonies.

The laws at first had little effect on the numbers of slaves taken from Africa to America. Certain countries, particularly Spain, Portugal, Cuba and Brazil were very slow to end the slave trade. In attempts to prevent slaving the British government signed treaties with several countries and also with rulers in West Africa and destroyed slave factories. (D20) Ships of the British and United States navies patrolled the Atlantic, chasing and stopping slave ships. Many of the slaves freed by the navy were landed at the West African settlement of Freetown and in Liberia. This is how these places got their names. Still the slave trade went on. Until the 1860s illegal slavers continued to slip in and out of the West African coast.

After 1840 the slave trade across the Atlantic fell rapidly. African states, such as Dahomey, which had depended for much of their wealth on the export of slaves to Europeans, now began to trade in other goods. The most important was palm oil which comes from the Guinea palm. The expanding industry of Western Europe and North America needed new supplies of oil for lubricating machinery, making soap, and as fuel for lamps. African rulers developed plantations of Guinea palms and instead of exporting slaves used them to produce oil for sale to European traders. In doing this they radically changed the old system of slavery in Africa and developed a new system of plantation slavery which in many ways was similar to that of America. European merchants who had grown rich by buying and selling of slaves now used steam ships to dominate much of this new source of trading wealth.

EMANCIPATION OF THE SLAVES

Although by 1830 many countries had forbidden the import or

Many blacks in the United States set up their own churches

A picture of Harlem, New York, showing how people who hoped to escape from poverty by moving to cities were often forced to live in slum conditions as bad as those which they had left

export of slaves it was still legal to own slaves in most European colonies and throughout North and South America. The fight to end slavery — to *emancipate* the slaves — lasted for most of the nineteenth century. The slaves in Britain's colonies (in the West Indies, South Africa and Mauritius) were freed after 1833; the French freed their slaves in 1848 and most South American countries in the 1850s.

But in the United States, Cuba and Brazil slavery continued. The slave owners were in powerful positions and needed the slaves to work the plantations which grew cotton, coffee and tobacco for export to Europe. The struggle for emancipation was long and bitter.

West Indians arriving in Britain to look for work in the 1950's

James Baldwin, the American Negro writer, was born in New York in 1924. He has always passionately supported the Negro cause in his novels and essays

The United States was split over the question of slavery. (D21) The rural southern States relied upon slave labour while in the northern states, where there was more manufacturing industry, slavery was illegal. The opponents of slavery helped slaves escape to the north; they held great meetings and ran newspapers. (D22) Finally, in 1861 the southern states broke away from the rest of the United States. A bloody civil war went on for four years before the northern states won. The slaves were freed.

Brazil had been built on slave labour. Opposition to slavery grew only after 1865. Slavery slowed up economic and political changes. Many Brazilians were against slavery because they wanted their country to be modern and democratic. Abolitionists encouraged slaves to run away from the plantations to the towns. The slave system collapsed in the 1880s and the slaves were finally freed.

In their colonies the Europeans still needed more workers. Sometimes they forced the local peasants to work for them. (D23) They also imported thousands of so-called *indentured labourers* – poor Indians and Chinese who signed Indentures (agreements) to work for long terms overseas. Today the descendants of those people live in countries such as South Africa, Malaysia, Fiji, Mauritius, and in the West Indies. (D24)

Freedom made little difference to the position of the black people in America. Most ex-slaves were poor and could easily be exploited and denied rights as citizens by the white majorities. A few blacks went to Liberia in West Africa (D25); others set up their own churches. Many more blacks hoped to escape from the poverty of the countryside by moving to the towns. In the United States they went to the northern industrial cities such as New York and Chicago; in Brazil they moved to coastal towns like Rio de Janeiro and Sao Paulo. Often they remained just as poor and lived in slum areas where only black people lived. The West Indian islands were desperately poor and were neglected by the whites who still governed them. After the Second World War thousands of people left the West Indies to find work and make new homes in Britain, France and the Netherlands. Many of the islands of the West Indies are now independent. In the United States in the last thirty years blacks have become more angry about the way in which they have been treated by the white majority. Black leaders have fought for new rights and opportunities for their people. (D26)

nationalist ideas of blacks in America have helped and influenced Africans struggling to gain their freedom from colonial rule. (D27)

But unpleasant jobs still exist and sometimes people are still forced to do them. Many countries still make people become soldiers. In the USSR people were made to work in the great labour camps in the frozen Arctic. Millions of people from conquered countries were forced to go and work in

THE EFFECTS OF THE SLAVE TRADE

The slave trade scattered millions of black people throughout the world, mainly to America but also to parts of Asia and Europe. This is its greatest effect. Africans suffered terribly from the slave trade. The youngest and best workers were sold into slavery, kings fought wars to get slaves, and the ways of life of whole communities were changed. The close contact of Africa with Europe also brought some trading advantages. New trade goods were introduced and important food crops such as maize from America.

The slaves took with them to America their languages, customs, music and beliefs. These have changed over the years but the African influence remains. Jazz and other popular movements in music throughout North and South America have sprung from African roots. Folk stories told in the West Indies have many links with those told in West Africa. And the

Marcus Garvey (1887-1940) was the founder of the Universal Negro Improvement Association, which aimed to unite Negroes all over the world, to gain economic power and to establish a black-governed nation in Africa

Germany during the Second World War. (D28) Indentured labour was a sort of voluntary slavery because men were legally bound to their jobs. Some men say that it is a sort of slavery when people are forced to do certain work because of hunger.

(D29) But this is not quite the same thing. If a man wants to leave his job there is no law which says he must stay. But when we think about these arguments it helps us to understand why slavery and the slave trade existed.

DOCUMENT 1

THE SLAVE SHIP   *OLAUDAH EQUIANO – An ex-slave who wrote his autobiography in 1789*

The first object I saw when I arrived on the coast was the sea, and a slave ship waiting for its cargo. When I was carried on board there was a multitude of black people of every description chained together, every one of their countenances expressing dejection and sorrow.

I was soon put under the decks, and there I received such a stench in my nostrils as I had never experienced in my life.

The closeness of the hold and the heat of the climate, added to the number in the ship, which was so crowded that each had scarcely room to turn itself, almost suffocated us. This wretched situation was again aggravated by the rubbing of the chains, now become insupportable, and the filth of the necessary tubs, into which the children often fell and were almost suffocated. The shrieks of the women and the groans of the dying rendered the whole a scene of horror almost inconceivable.

DOCUMENT 2

ADVICE TO THE SLAVE OWNER   *MARCUS TERENTIUS VARRO – A Roman writer*

Slaves should be neither timorous nor high-spirited. Their foremen should know how to read and write and have some little education . . . They are not to be permitted to control their men with whips rather than with words, so long as you can achieve the same result. Avoid having too many slaves of the same nation, for this is a regular source of domestic quarrels . . . You must win the good-will of the foremen by treating them with some consideration, and also those of the hands who excel the others should be consulted about the work to be done: when this happens, they are less inclined to think that they are looked down upon, and rather think that they are held in some esteem by their master. You can make them more interested in their work by treating them more liberally so far as food or clothing are concerned, or exemption from work; or by allowing them to graze some cattle of their own on the farm, or other things of this kind.

DOCUMENT 3

MALIK AMBAR   *JAHANGIR — The Mughal Emperor writing of the
black ex-slave who became a great military leader and fought the
Mughal emperors in Central India in the seventeenth century*

Malik Ambar, whether as a commander or strategist, was without equal
in military art. He kept the rabble of Central India in perfect order and
to the end of his days lived in honour. There is no record elsewhere in
history of an African slave attaining to such a position as was held by
him.

DOCUMENT 4

AN ARAB VIEW OF BLACK MEN   *JAHIZ OF BASRA — A great
Arab writer in the 8th Century A.D.*

We know that the Zanj (Africans) are the least intelligent and the least
discerning of mankind, and the least capable of understanding the
consequences of actions . . .
    The like of the crow among mankind are the Zanj for they are the
worst of men and the most vicious of creatures in character and
temperament . . . they have boundless stupidity . . . and evil dispositions.

DOCUMENT 5

LANDING SLAVES IN EUROPE   *A Portuguese writer in the
fifteenth century describes the arrival of black slaves at Lisbon*

Some slaves kept their heads low and their faces bathed in tears, looking
one upon another; others stood groaning, looking up to heaven, crying
out loudly; others struck their faces with the palms of their hands,
throwing themselves at full length upon the ground. But to increase their
sufferings still more, there now arrived those who had charge of the
division of the captives, and who began to separate one from another;
and then was it needful to part fathers from sons, husbands from wives,
brothers from brothers. No respect was shewn either to friends or
relations, but each fell where his lot took him.

DOCUMENT 6

A PROTEST AGAINST SLAVING   *NZINGA MVEMBA – The Christian King of Kongo (1506-43) protests to the King of Portugal about the slave trade*

Sir, many of our people, keenly desirous of the wares and things of your kingdoms, which are brought here by your many people, and in order to satisfy their greed, seize many of our free people; and very often it happens that they kidnap even noblemen and the sons of noblemen, and our relatives, and take them to be sold to the white men who are in our kingdoms . . . And to avoid such a great evil we passed a law so that any white man living in our Kingdoms and wanting to purchase goods in any way should first inform three of our noblemen and officials of our court . . . who should investigate if the mentioned goods are captives or free men.

DOCUMENT 7

A SLAVE CARAVAN   *MUNGO PARK – The explorer who travelled on a forty-four day, five hundred mile journey with a slave caravan in 1796*

The slaves which Karfa had brought with him were all of them prisoners of war . . . they viewed me at first with looks of horror, and repeatedly asked if my countrymen were cannibals. A deeply rooted idea, that the whites purchase Negroes for the purpose of eating them, or of selling them to others, that they may be eaten, makes the slaves contemplate a journey towards the Coast with great terror; insomuch that the merchants are forced to keep them constantly in irons, and watch them very closely, to prevent their escape. They are commonly secured by putting the right leg of one and the left of another, into the same pair of fetters. By supporting the fetters with a string, they can walk, though very slowly. Every four slaves are likewise fastened together by the necks, with a strong rope of twisted thongs; and in the night, an additional pair of fetters is put on their hands, and sometimes a light chain passed round their necks.

DOCUMENT 8

BUYING SLAVES IN WEST AFRICA   *WILLIAM BOSMAN – A slave trader, describing the buying of slaves at Whydah in this letter to his uncle*

When these slaves come to Whydah they are put in Prison all together, and when we treat concerning buying them, they are all brought out together in a large Plain; where, by our surgeons, they are thoroughly examined,

24

even to the smallest member, and that naked too both men and women, without the least distinction or modesty. Those which are approved as good are set on one side; and the lame or faulty are set by as invalids.

The invalids and the maimed being thrown out, the remainder are numbered, and it is entered who delivered them. In the meanwhile a burning iron, with the arms or name of the companies, lies in the fire; with which ours are marked on the breast.

This is done that we may distinguish them from the slaves of the English, French or others.

I doubt not but this trade seems very barbarous to you, but since it is followed by mere necessity it must go on; but we yet take all possible care that they are not burned too hard, especially the women, who are more tender than the men.

When we have agreed with the owners of the slaves, they are returned to their prison where they subsist, like our criminals, on bread and water: so that to save charges we send them on board our ships with the very first opportunity; before which their masters strip them of all they have on their backs; so that they come aboard stark-naked as well women as men:

You would really wonder to see how these slaves live on board; for though their number sometimes amounts to six or seven hundred, yet by the careful management of our masters of ships, they are so regulated that it seems incredible.

The slaves are fed three times a day with good food, and much better than they eat in their own country. Their lodging-place is divided into two parts; one of which is appointed for the men the other for the women; each sex being kept apart: here they lie as close together as is possible for them to be crowded.

DOCUMENT 9

THE SLAVE TRADE AND BRITISH PROSPERITY
MALACHI POSTLETHWAYT — In his *African Trade, the Great Pillar and Support of the British Plantation Trade in North America, 1745*

But is it not well-known that the business of planting in our British Colonies, as well as in the French, is carried on by the labour of negroes, imported from Africa? Are we not indebted to the Africans, for our sugar, tobacco, rice, rum, and all other plantation produce? And the greater the number of negroes imported into our colonies, from Africa, will not the exportation of British manufactures among the Africans be in proportion; they being paid for in such commodities only? The more our plantations abound in negroes, will not more land become cultivated, and both better and greater variety of plantation commodities be produced? May we not therefore say . . . that the general navigation of Great Britain owes all its increase and splendour to the commerce of its

American and African colonies; and that it cannot be maintained and enlarged otherwise than from the constant prosperity of both those branches, whose interests are mutual and inseparable?

DOCUMENT 10

NEWSPAPER ADVERTISEMENT   *NEW ORLEANS BEE — A*
nineteenth century newspaper

NEGROES FOR SALE — A negro woman, twenty-four years of age, and her two children, one eight and the other three years old. Said negroes will be sold SEPARATELY or together, *as desired.* The woman is a good seamstress. She will be sold low for cash, or EXCHANGED FOR GROCERIES. For terms, apply to MATTHEW BLISS & CO., 1 Front Levee.

DOCUMENT 11

RELIGION AND SLAVERY   *A sermon to slaves by a bishop of*
Virginia, eighteenth century

Almighty God hath been pleased to make you slaves here, and give you nothing but labour and poverty in this world, which you are obliged to submit to as it is His will that it should be so. Your bodies, you know, are not your own: they are at the disposal of those who you belong to.

DOCUMENT 12

PLANTATION LABOUR IN THE UNITED STATES
SOLOMON NORTHUP in his *Twelve Years a Slave, 1854*

An hour before daylight the horn is blown. Then the slaves arouse, prepare their breakfast, fill a gourd with water, in another, deposit their dinner of cold bacon and corn cake, and hurry to the field again. It is an offense invariably followed by a flogging to be found at the quarters after daybreak. Then the fears and labours of another day begin and until its close there is no such thing as rest.

. . . with the exception of ten or fifteen minutes, which is given them at noon to swallow their allowance of cold bacon, they are not permitted to be a moment idle until it is too dark to see, and when the moon is full, they oftentimes labour till the middle of the night. They do not dare to stop even at dinner time, nor return to the quarters, however late it be, until the order to halt is given by the driver.

DOCUMENT 13

SLAVE LABOUR IN BRAZIL *THOMAS NELSON – An Englishman visiting Brazil in the nineteenth Century*

The negro is not only the field labourer, but also the mechanic; not only hews the wood and draws the water, but by the skill of his hands contributes to fashion the luxuries of civilized life. The Brazilian employs him on all occasions, and in every possible way; – from fulfilling the office of valet and cook, to serving the purposes of the horse; from forming the gaudy trinkets, and shaping the costume which is to clothe and decorate his person, to discharging the vilest of servile duties.

DOCUMENT 14

THE NEGRO STATE OF PALMARES *FERNAO CARRILHO – A Portuguese soldier writing about the two military expeditions he had led against the black republic of Palmares between 1672 and 1680*

The king of Palmares is called *Ganga-Zumba,* which means Great Lord; he has a large palace and he is assisted by guards and officials. He is treated with all respect due to a monarch. Those who are in his presence kneel on the ground and strike palm leaves with their hands as a sign of appreciation of his excellence. The capital of Palmares is fortified with parapets. There are keepers of the law. Although these barbarians have all but forgotten the Church they still have a chapel and images to which they direct their worship. There are other towns in charge of which are major chiefs. The second city in importance is called Subupuira and is ruled by the king's brother. It has 800 houses. It is here that Negroes are trained to fight our assaults and weapons are forged there.

DOCUMENT 15

NAT TURNER'S REBELLION *Inspired by the Old Testament, Nat Turner led a slave revolt in Southampton County, Virginia, in 1831*

I heard a loud noise in the heavens and the Spirit instantly appeared to me and said that I should fight against the serpent (the whites).
I took my station in the rear and, as it was my object to carry terror and devastation wherever we went, I placed fifteen or twenty of the best armed and most to be relied on in front, who generally approached the houses as fast as their horses could run. This was for two purposes – to prevent their escape, and strike terror into the inhabitants.

DOCUMENT 16

HAITI'S INDEPENDENCE   *TOUSSAINT L'OUVERTURE — In this letter to Napoleon in 1801, he defends the right of Haiti to decide its own affairs*

You say in your letter that Haiti . . . is showing a tendency to independence. Why should this not be so? The United States of America did exactly that; and with the assistance of France, succeeded . . . The high post which I hold is not of my choosing . . . The power which I hold has been as legitimately acquired as your own, and nothing but the expressed wish of the people of Haiti will force me to give it up.

DOCUMENT 17

A VOICE AGAINST SLAVERY   *MARQUIS DE CONDORCET — The French thinker who opposed slavery. Author of 'Reflections on Negro Slavery' 1788*

My friends: although I am not of your colour, I have always regarded you as my brothers. Nature has endowed you with the same mind, the same reason, the same virtues as the whites . . . I know how often your loyalty, your honesty, your courage have made your masters blush. If one wished to find a man in the isles of America, it would not be among the people of white skin that one would find him.

DOCUMENT 18

UNPROFITABLE LABOUR   *ADAM SMITH — A Scottish political economist and philosopher writing in his book 'The Wealth of Nations' that Britain's industry and trade needed to be free of restrictions*

The experience of all ages and nations, I believe, demonstrates that the work done by slaves, though it appears to cost only their maintenance, is in the end the dearest of any. A person who can acquire no property, can have no other interest but to eat as much, and to labour as little as possible. Whatever work he does beyond what is sufficient to purchase his own maintenance can be squeezed out of him by violence only . . .

DOCUMENT 19

OPPOSITION TO THE SLAVE TRADE   *THOMAS CLARKSON — One of the leaders of the British Anti-slavery Society who wrote 'On the Slavery and Commerce of the Human Species', 1786*

. . . by incessant labour the continual application of the lash, and the most inhuman treatment that imagination can devise, you overwhelm the

genius of the African and hinder it from breaking forth . . . The
unfortunate Africans . . . have no hope of riches, power, honours, fame.
They have no hope but this, that their miseries will be soon terminated
by death . . . the wretched Africans are torn from their country for as
long as slavery continues.

DOCUMENT 20

BRITISH DESTRUCTION OF SLAVE FACTORIES IN WEST AFRICA,
1849   *In an attempt to stop the slave trade the British African
Squadron attacked and destroyed the trading factories on the West
African coast. A British Commodore writes to the Admiralty.*

On the 3rd I assembled my seven ships off Gallinas, and with a force of
300 men landed at Dombocorro, took possession of it, and the neighbour-
ing factories and barracoons (slave pens), and planted sentinels to guard
the property. In the meantime, Captain Jones pushed on to the Solyman
factories which, along with the village of Dreesing, known for its intimate
connection with the slave trade, he totally destroyed. On the following
morning the large factories in the vicinity of Dombocorro were, with the
goods which they contained, entirely destroyed; and at 1 pm on the same
day, Dombocorro itself, with all its contents was burnt to the ground.

DOCUMENT 21

IN DEFENCE OF SLAVERY   *JOHN CALHOUN (1782-1850)* –
A southern slave-holder who believed that slavery was a 'positive good'

We of the South will not, cannot surrender our institutions. To maintain
the existing relations between the two races . . . is indispensable to the
peace and happiness of both. Slaveholding I hold to be a good. Never
before has the black race of Africa attained a condition so civilised and
so improved, not only physically, but morally and intellectually. It came
here among us in a low, degraded, and savage condition, and in the course
of a few generations it has grown up under the fostering care of our
institutions . . . to its present civilised condition. I hold that in the
present state of civilisation, where two races of different origin, and
distinguished by colour, and other physical differences, as well as
intellectual, are brought together, the relation now existing in the slaveholding States between the two, is, instead of an evil, a good – a positive
good.

DOCUMENT 22

A MILITANT BLACK VOICE AGAINST SLAVERY
HENRY GARNET (1815-82) — A former slave, arguing that slaves should use violence to win their freedom

Brethren, it is as wrong for your lordly oppressors to keep you in slavery as it was for the man thief to steal our ancestors from the coast of Africa. You should therefore now use the same manner of resistance as would have been just in our ancestors when the bloody foot-prints of that first thief were placed upon the shores of our fatherland . . .
Brethren, arise, arise! Strike for your lives and liberties. You cannot be more oppressed than you have been — you cannot suffer greater cruelties than you have already. *Rather die free men than live to be slaves.*
Remember that you are FOUR MILLIONS! Let your motto be resistance! Resistance! RESISTANCE!

DOCUMENT 23

FORCED LABOUR IN THE CONGO FREE STATE
EDMOND PICARD — A Belgian M.P. who visited the Congo in 1906 describes the situation in the country which was the vast private estate of King Leopold of Belgium. Africans were forced to collect rubber and ivory.

I saw a continual procession of blacks, carrying loads upon their heads; worn-out beasts of burden, with projecting joints, wasted features, and staring eyes . . . By thousands they are in the service of the State . . . There are inhuman floggings, murders, plunderings . . .

DOCUMENT 24

INDENTURED LABOUR IN TRINIDAD   *SIR HENRY ALCAZAR —*
The Mayor of Port-of-Spain, Trinidad giving evidence to the West India Royal Commission in 1897, describing the effects of the bringing of half a million indentured labourers to the Caribbean islands by the British, French and Dutch between 1840 and 1910

On his employer . . . the effect is much more similar to that of slavery, for if one fifth of his bondsmen are set free every year, a fresh fifth at once takes their place, and he has permanently about him a large number of his fellow men bound to do his bidding under penalty of imprisonment. In fact, with regard to its effect of the employer, the system is not very different from slavery, with the jail substituted for the whip. And one of the worst consequences of Indian immigration in Trinidad has been to keep its educated classes at the moral level of slave owners.

DOCUMENT 25

BACK TO AFRICA   *BISHOP HENRY TURNER (1834-1915) –*
The black leader of the African Methodist Episcopal Church in the
United States urging Negroes to go back to Africa

I see nothing for the Negro to attain in this country . . . He can return to
Africa, especially to Liberia where a Negro government is already in
existence, and learn the elements of civilization in fact . . . there is
nothing in the United States for the Negro to learn or try to attain to . . .
   Yes, I would make Africa a place of refuge, because I see no other
shelter from the stormy blast, from the red tide of persecution, from the
horrors of American prejudice.

DOCUMENT 26

BLACK PROTEST FOR CIVIL RIGHTS
REV. MARTIN LUTHER KING – The black leader, who was
imprisoned in Birmingham, Alabama, in 1963 for leading a black
protest march, here arguing for non-violent protests

I stand in the middle of two opposing forces in the Negro community.
One is the force of complacency made up of Negroes who have been so
completely drained of self-respect that they have adjusted to segregation
and those Negroes who profit by segregation. The other force is one of
bitterness and hatred . . . It is expressed in the various black nationalist
groups, the largest and best known being Elijah Muhammad's Muslim
Movement. This movement is nourished by the frustration over the
continued existence of racial discrimination. I have tried to stand
between these two forces saying there is a more excellent way of love
and non-violent protest. If this philosophy had not emerged I am
convinced that by now many streets of the South would be flowing with
floods of blood.

DOCUMENT 27

BLACK NATIONALISM   *MARCUS GARVEY – A Jamaican, who*
in 1914 organized the Universal Negro Improvement Association in
New York, here talking to a large meeting in 1920

The Negroes of the world say, 'We are striking homewards towards Africa
to make the big black republic'. And in the making of Africa a big black
republic, what is the barrier? The barrier is the white man; and we say to
the white man who now dominates Africa that it is to his interest to clear
out of Africa now, because . . . we are coming 400,000,000 strong, and
we mean to retake every square inch of the twelve million square miles
of African territory belonging to us by right Divine . . . We are out to get
what has belonged to us politically, economically, and in every way.

DOCUMENT 28

FORCED LABOUR AT THE KRUPP WORKS, ESSEN, GERMANY, 1944 *Evidence taken at Nuremberg War Crimes Tribunal, 1946*

The camp inmates were mostly Jewish women and girls from Hungary and Rumania. They were brought to Essen at the beginning of 1944 and were put to work at Krupps. The accommodation and feeding of the camp prisoners was beneath all dignity.
. . . Reveille was at 5 am. There was no coffee or any food served in the morning. They marched off to the factory at 5.15 am. They marched for three-quarters of an hour to the factory, poorly clothed and badly shod, some without shoes, and, in rain or snow, covered in a blanket. Work began at 6 am. Lunch break was from 12 to 12.30. Only during the break was it at all possible for the prisoners to cook something for themselves from potato peelings and other garbage. The daily working period was one of from ten to eleven hours. The prisoners were often maltreated at their work-benches by Nazi overseers and female SS guards.

DOCUMENT 29

MODERN SLAVERY IN ARABIA *A German traveller talks with*
Il Grandone, an African slave in modern Arabia, 1964

I spoke to Il Grandone in Italian. The big Negro came from the former Italian Eritrea and although he was a Mohammedan he had learnt to read and write from the Italian missionaries, and from them had got the name Il Grandone (the giant). On a pilgrimage to Mecca he had fallen into debt and was compelled to sell himself. The irresistible question at once sprang to my lips: 'Would you not rather be free?' to which he replied, 'I have a good master.'
    'The Europeans', he said quietly 'cannot understand slavery because they do not know the Arabs, nor do they know what real poverty is. Certainly in Europe with you I should want to be free as you, but in Africa or here — no. I am far better off as a slave. If I am sick my master calls a doctor; I get regular meals and a little money. If I do something wrong he protects me from the police. Who bothers about a free man and especially about a poor free man? He has no doctor, no free penicillin and not even enough to eat. What is such freedom worth? Nothing at all, I tell you. We slaves live much longer than the poor: yes, much longer.'

ACKNOWLEDGMENTS

Camera Press pages 19 (top), 20; Mansell Collection pages 2, 4, 8 (top), 13, 15, 16 (top), 17 (top); Mary Evans Picture Library pages 7, 8 (bottom), 12, 16 (bottom), 17 (bottom); Radio Times Hulton Picture Library pages 5, 14 (both pictures), 18, 19 (bottom); United Press International (U.K.) Ltd page 21.

Greenhaven World History Program

History Makers
Alexander
Constantine
Leonardo Da Vinci
Columbus
Luther, Erasmus and Loyola
Napoleon
Bolivar
Adam Smith, Malthus and Marx
Darwin
Bismark
Henry Ford
Roosevelt
Stalin
Mao Tse-Tung
Gandhi
Nyerere and Nkrumah

Great Civilizations
The Ancient Near East
Ancient Greece
Pax Romana
The Middle Ages
Spices and Civilization
Chingis Khan and the Mongol Empire
Akbar and the Mughal Empire
Traditional China
Ancient America
Traditional Africa
Asoka and Indian Civilization
Mohammad and the Arab Empire
Ibin Sina and the Muslim World
Suleyman and the Ottoman Empire

Great Revolutions
The Neolithic Revolution
The Agricultural Revolution
The Scientific Revolution
The Industrial Revolution
The Communications Revolution
The American Revolution
The French Revolution
The Mexican Revolution
The Russian Revolution
The Chinese Revolution

Enduring Issues
Cities
Population
Health and Wealth
A World Economy
Law
Religion
Language
Education
The Family

Political and Social Movements
The Slave Trade
The Enlightenment
Imperialism
Nationalism
The British Raj and Indian Nationalism
The Growth of the State
The Suez Canal
The American Frontier
Japan's Modernization
Hitler's Reich
The Two World Wars
The Atom Bomb
The Cold War
The Wealth of Japan
Hollywood